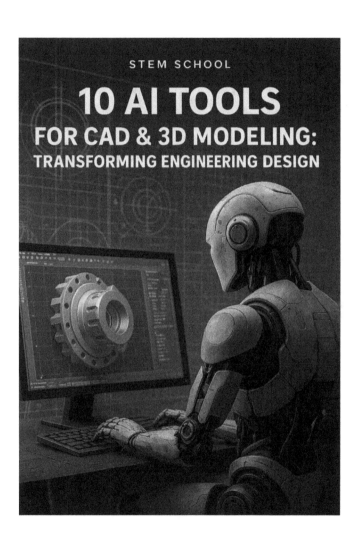

STEM SCHOOL

10 AI TOOLS

FOR CAD & 3D MODELING:

TRANSFORMING ENGINEERING DESIGN

10 AI Tools for CAD & 3D Modeling

Transforming Engineering Design

By

STEM School

This Page Left Intentionally Blank

Contents

Introduction

The Rise of AI in CAD and 3D Modeling

In recent years, Artificial Intelligence (AI) has become one of the most transformative technologies in the field of computer-aided design (CAD) and 3D modeling. Traditionally, CAD and 3D modeling relied on manual inputs, geometric reasoning, and rules predefined by human designers. Engineers would spend hours crafting technical drawings, iterating through countless versions, and checking compliance with design specifications. However, with the emergence of AI-driven tools, this process is undergoing a radical shift—moving from a human-centered approach to a human-AI collaborative workflow.

AI in the context of CAD and 3D modeling does not simply refer to automation or parametric design. It represents a deeper integration of machine learning, generative design, computer vision, natural language processing, and predictive analytics into the engineering workflow. These technologies allow systems to learn from past designs, predict design flaws before they occur, generate new geometries optimized for weight, strength, and material usage, and even interact with designers using plain human language.

As industries push for faster development cycles, leaner production processes, and personalized products at scale, the need for intelligent design systems becomes undeniable. AI meets these demands by enabling systems to "understand" and "adapt" to design requirements, often reducing what once took weeks into a matter of hours—or even minutes.

The relationship between AI and CAD is not just a case of adding smart features. It is about redefining how engineers and designers think about creating objects, buildings, systems, and machines. Instead of acting as mere operators, designers now collaborate with AI models that propose alternatives, test scenarios, and recommend optimizations. The AI acts not as a tool, but as a partner in innovation.

Transforming Engineering Design

The fusion of AI with engineering design and manufacturing has launched the industry into what many refer to as Industry 4.0—a smart, connected, and data-driven era. In design, AI enables generative modeling, topology optimization, and design validation in real time. These capabilities mean that instead of relying solely on trial and error or finite element analysis after a model is created, designers can now let algorithms explore thousands of design iterations based on objectives like minimizing weight, maximizing airflow, or reducing material cost. The result is often a highly efficient and innovative design that would be nearly impossible to create using traditional methods.

In manufacturing, AI integrates with CAD tools to anticipate production issues. For example, AI can analyze a 3D model and detect whether a part is manufacturable using CNC machining, additive manufacturing (3D printing), or injection molding. It can flag areas with thin walls, overhangs, or undercuts that might cause complications. Furthermore, AI-powered quality control systems are increasingly used to inspect finished parts through visual data analysis, improving consistency and reducing scrap rates.

AI also plays a critical role in supply chain optimization and production scheduling. Once a product is designed, intelligent systems can predict delivery timelines, estimate production costs with greater accuracy, and suggest suppliers based on part specifications and geographic constraints. This level of integration between design and production shortens time-to-market and creates a seamless feedback loop that drives continuous improvement.

What This Book Offers to the Reader

This book is designed to provide a comprehensive yet practical guide to understanding and leveraging AI in CAD and 3D modeling. Whether you're a student, a hobbyist, a mechanical engineer, or a product designer, this book will help you understand the tools, technologies, and strategies shaping the future of design and production. Each chapter aims to build not only technical knowledge but also strategic insight, giving you the confidence to use AI as part of your daily workflow.

Readers will start with foundational concepts such as machine learning, neural networks, and AI workflows in design environments. From there, we will explore real-world use cases where AI has enhanced traditional CAD processes. You will learn how to create generative designs, conduct AI-driven simulations, implement natural language interfaces in modeling software, and build predictive models that support design decision-making.

The book also includes case studies from industries like aerospace, automotive, architecture, and consumer electronics to show how companies are using AI to achieve lighter parts, faster prototyping, better ergonomics, and reduced production costs. Furthermore, it will provide access to open-source tools, code snippets, and AI modeling platforms that readers can experiment with on their own. A key feature of this book is the step-by-step project plans that walk you through building AI-enhanced models. These projects are accompanied by detailed explanations, timelines, and SMART goals that ensure you are not only learning theory but applying it in real-world scenarios.]The table below outlines the types of content you can expect across various chapters

Chapter	Focus Area	Key Skills Developed	Tools Covered
1	AI Fundamentals for Designers	Understanding ML, AI, neural networks	TensorFlow, Python, Scikit-learn
2	Generative Design Techniques	Creating optimized geometries with AI	Autodesk Fusion 360, SolidWorks
3	Natural Language	Voice and text-based control of	ChatGPT, Rhino +

Chapter	Focus Area	Key Skills Developed	Tools Covered
	Interfaces in CAD	CAD tools	Grasshopper
4	Predictive Modeling for Manufacturing	Anticipating defects, cost, and performance	MATLAB, PTC Creo, SimScale
5	AI-Powered Quality Control	Computer vision, defect detection	OpenCV, Deep Learning models
6	Real-World Projects and Case Studies	Application in aerospace, consumer products	Blender, FreeCAD, Revit

By the end of this book, readers will not only understand the theory behind AI in CAD and 3D modeling, but they will also be capable of implementing real-world AI solutions that can transform how they design and manufacture products. In essence, this book is more than a guide—it's a roadmap to the future of engineering design. AI is not here to replace human creativity. Instead, it enhances it, providing new tools and capabilities that allow designers to focus on what truly matters solving problems, innovating solutions, and building the next generation of products that shape the world.

Chapter 1

Parametric Design with Autodesk Fusion 360

Autodesk Fusion 360 stands at the forefront of next-generation computer-aided design software, offering a robust suite of AI-driven capabilities that are transforming how engineers, designers, and manufacturers approach product development. As a cloud-based CAD, CAM, and CAE tool, Fusion 360 seamlessly integrates mechanical design, electronics, simulation, and collaboration into a unified platform. Its recent advancements in artificial intelligence have elevated the design process from a series of manual tasks into an intelligent, responsive, and automated experience.

One of the most powerful ways AI shows up in Fusion 360 is through its **generative design engine**, which uses machine learning algorithms and cloud computing to produce multiple high-performance design alternatives based on user-defined constraints and goals. Rather than sculpting geometry manually, users can now guide the software by specifying performance criteria such as strength, weight, materials, and cost—and let the AI explore and propose thousands of possible configurations.

Fusion 360's AI capabilities also include **design automation**, **adaptive toolpaths**, and **data-driven manufacturing simulation**. These features work together to minimize human error, shorten design cycles, and enhance the quality and performance of final products. This makes it an ideal environment for both beginners and professionals looking to explore the future of AI-assisted parametric design.

Parametric Modeling with AI Assistance

Parametric modeling has long been a foundation of CAD, allowing users to create geometry driven by variables and relationships instead of fixed dimensions. In Fusion 360, parametric modeling is enhanced by intelligent systems that learn from user behavior, suggest common constraints, and auto-adjust linked dimensions to preserve design intent.

What makes this even more powerful is the integration of AI, especially through the **Generative Design Workspace**. While traditional parametric modeling requires the designer to make every modeling decision—from the location of holes to the curvature of fillets—AI-assisted generative modeling shifts the approach entirely. Instead of dictating the form, users define the problem.

For example, in a bracket design, you might specify the locations where loads are applied, the areas where material is restricted, the required safety factor, and the target material (such as aluminum or titanium). Once these goals and constraints are defined, Fusion 360's AI engine processes the inputs and produces a wide range of viable design options, each optimized for the chosen parameters. These designs are not random; they are mathematically and physically validated using built-in simulation tools, offering solutions that are both feasible and performance-optimized.

The image below conceptually illustrates how generative design differs from traditional CAD

Diagram Traditional vs. AI-Driven Design

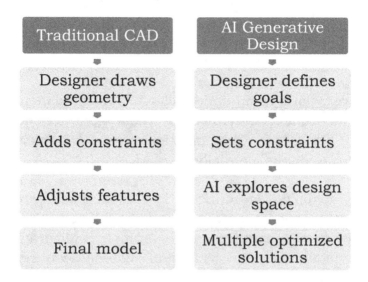

Automating Design Variations with AI

One of the most practical uses of AI in Fusion 360 is the automation of design variations. In product design, it is often necessary to test multiple versions of a component— whether to accommodate different use cases, meet client requirements, or optimize for material use. Doing this manually would be time-consuming and error-prone.

Fusion 360 offers a **Design of Experiments (DOE)** approach using AI. When creating parameters in the Parameters dialog, users can link variables such as thickness, hole diameter, or length. By combining this with **Scripts and Add-Ins** or using the **Generative Design**

Preview, it becomes possible to generate families of parts automatically. AI learns which parameters most significantly affect outcomes like structural integrity, weight, or printability, and can recommend optimal values or warn about poor combinations.

Moreover, cloud computation allows AI to simulate multiple variations concurrently, making it feasible to test dozens— or even hundreds—of combinations within a fraction of the time it would take manually.

This capability is critical in fields like aerospace, automotive, and consumer electronics where a single part may need to be manufactured in multiple configurations, or where reducing a few grams of material can result in significant cost savings across millions of units.

Create an AI-Generated Mechanical Part

To understand the practical power of AI in Fusion 360, let's walk through a hands-on example of creating an AI-generated mechanical part using generative design. In this exercise, we will design a **lightweight mounting bracket** optimized for strength and material use.

Step 1 Define the Design Problem

Open Fusion 360 and switch to the **Generative Design Workspace**. Begin by setting up your study.

- Create a base sketch for the bracket's mounting interface.

- Define **preserved geometry**—this is the region where the bracket must remain solid, such as holes for bolts or contact areas.
- Define **obstacle geometry**—these are the zones where material is restricted or should not appear.

Step 2 Apply Loads and Constraints

Apply static loads at the points where the bracket would experience force in real-world use, such as a downward force at the end of the bracket arm. Fix one face of the bracket to simulate wall attachment. Set a target **safety factor**, such as 2.0.

Step 3 Choose Materials and Objectives

Select the materials the AI can use, such as 6061 Aluminum, Stainless Steel, or Nylon (for additive manufacturing). Then set the optimization goals—minimize mass while maintaining structural strength.

Step 4 Generate Design Options

Click "Generate" and allow Fusion 360 to run the simulation on the cloud. You will receive a gallery of optimized shapes, each meeting your performance criteria. These may look organic or skeletal in form—aesthetic that would be hard for a human to envision without assistance.

Step 5 Export the Design

Select your preferred design, convert it to a solid BREP (Boundary Representation), and return to the **Design Workspace** to finalize it with mounting features, fillets, or manufacturing tolerances.

Timeline and SMART Goals

Week	Goal	SMART Objective
1	Learn Fusion 360 basics	Complete tutorials on parametric modeling by the end of the first week
2	Understand generative design interface	Launch your first generative study with defined goals and constraints
3	Create your AI-optimized bracket	Export at least 3 design iterations based on performance goals
4	Evaluate and test designs	Simulate stress and material use for each design to choose the best performer

This chapter has provided a deep dive into the capabilities of Autodesk Fusion 360 as a leader in AI-powered design tools. You have seen how generative design changes the role of the engineer from geometry creator to design strategist—someone who defines problems, sets objectives, and evaluates solutions. Through parametric modeling, automated variation, and hands-on projects, AI allows anyone—from students to professionals—to harness vast computational power and design with greater intelligence, speed, and innovation. As you move forward through this book, the principles introduced here will continue to build into more advanced applications of AI in simulation, manufacturing, and real-world problem solving. Embrace the transition, and let AI enhance your creative potential in the world of engineering design.

Chapter 2

Design with Autodesk Inventor & AI

Autodesk Inventor, traditionally known for parametric modeling and mechanical design, has in recent years adopted intelligent, AI-enhanced tools that are reshaping how engineers create optimized components. One of the most transformative features now embedded into the design ecosystem is **generative design**, a method that fundamentally redefines the way parts are conceptualized and manufactured.

At its core, generative design within Autodesk Inventor integrates advanced simulation, topology optimization, and machine learning algorithms to generate performance-optimized geometries based on specific user-defined constraints. Rather than asking the designer to sculpt every contour manually, Inventor's AI algorithms use performance objectives—such as minimum weight, maximum rigidity, material usage efficiency, and stress constraints—to explore a wide solution space. The result is not a single static design but a set of algorithmically optimized, structurally efficient alternatives.

Inventor achieves this through a tight integration with Autodesk's cloud computing and simulation technologies, particularly when paired with Fusion Team or Autodesk Vault for collaborative environments. The process enables rapid iteration and enables users to compare options based on mechanical performance, manufacturing cost, and material sustainability.

The diagram below outlines how the generative design workflow functions in Inventor when enhanced by AI

Diagram AI Generative Workflow in Autodesk Inventor

Topology Optimization and Weight Reduction

One of the most tangible benefits of AI-driven generative design in Autodesk Inventor is the ability to conduct **topology optimization**. This is a process where AI systematically removes unnecessary material from a part while ensuring that the final structure maintains its strength and stiffness under expected load conditions.

In traditional design, engineers would over-engineer parts to ensure safety margins, often resulting in components that are heavier, bulkier, and more expensive than necessary. AI eliminates this inefficiency by mathematically analyzing stress paths and redistributing material only where it is functionally required. This process is especially valuable when designing parts for industries where **weight reduction** is critical—such as aerospace, automotive, and robotics.

In Autodesk Inventor, topology optimization is accessible through the Shape Generator tool. Here, users can define fixed points, force directions, material properties, and safety factors. The software then simulates various design conditions and returns an optimized mesh or body that can be further refined and turned into manufacturable geometry.

To illustrate the impact of topology optimization, consider a simple load-bearing bracket. Without optimization, it might weigh 800 grams. After AI-driven generative design and topology refinement, the bracket could weigh just 250 grams while performing equally well under structural tests. This results in significant material savings, lower carbon footprint, and reduced shipping or fuel costs.

A conceptual example is shown below

Diagram Weight Optimization of a Bracket

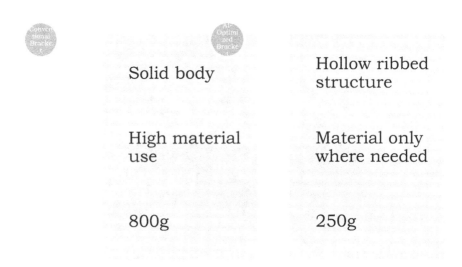

Solid body	Hollow ribbed structure
High material use	Material only where needed
800g	250g

Real-World Industrial Applications

The influence of generative design and AI-driven optimization is not theoretical—it is already being implemented across several industries with transformative outcomes. In the **aerospace sector**, companies such as Airbus and Boeing have adopted generative design to reduce the weight of aircraft components, leading to lower fuel consumption and reduced emissions over the lifespan of an aircraft. For example, a single lightweight bracket optimized using generative design can save up to half a kilogram. When multiplied by thousands of parts in a single aircraft, the cumulative savings become massive.

Similarly, in the **automotive industry**, manufacturers like General Motors and BMW are using generative design to improve the structural integrity of car frames, suspension parts, and engine mounts while reducing mass. This enables vehicles to become more energy efficient and improves overall performance. Generative parts often have an organic, lattice-like appearance that would be almost impossible to create using conventional design methods. Fortunately, advancements in additive manufacturing, particularly 3D metal printing, now allow for the fabrication of these complex geometries.

In both industries, generative design does not just optimize the physical component; it enhances the entire lifecycle of a product—from development to recycling—by embedding sustainability into the early stages of the design process.

The following table summarizes real-world benefits of AI-driven generative design across key sectors

Table Industry Benefits of Generative Design with AI

Industry	Application	Benefit	Impact on Manufacturing
Aerospace	Aircraft brackets and seat supports	Up to 55% weight reduction	Lower fuel use, reduced emissions
Automotive	Engine mounts, suspension arms	Enhanced strength with 40% less material	Better fuel economy, faster design
Robotics	Lightweight frames and joints	Compact and modular designs	Improved agility and payload capacity
Medical Devices	Custom implants and prosthetics	Patient-specific optimization	More comfort, better healing

Lightweight Bracket Design with AI

To bring the concepts of this chapter into practical application, let's walk through a hands-on project in Autodesk Inventor focused on designing a lightweight bracket using generative design principles and AI-powered optimization.

Project Objective Design a wall-mounted bracket that supports a 300 N load, minimizes weight, and is suitable for aluminum fabrication using generative design.

Step 1 Setup and Constraints

Launch Autodesk Inventor and create a new part file. Begin by sketching the preserved regions—these represent the bolt mounting holes and load contact points. Use precise dimensions and locate these points according to your intended real-world use.

Next, enter the **Shape Generator** environment. Define the preserved regions and apply **fixed constraints** at the mounting points. Apply a **downward force of 300 N** at the location where the bracket will carry load. Ensure the material is set to **6061 Aluminum**, and define a **safety factor of 2.0**.

Step 2 Generate Shape and Analyze

Run the topology optimization simulation. Inventor will analyze the structure and return an optimized mesh showing the ideal material distribution. You will notice that material is retained only along essential load paths, resulting in a skeletal or ribbed appearance.

Use the mesh as a reference and begin redesigning your model to closely match the suggested topology. Add fillets, cutouts, and manufacturable features. Save and proceed to simulate the final model under the same load conditions using the **Stress Analysis** environment.

Step 3 Evaluate Results and Iterate

Compare the results with your original solid bracket design. Measure weight reduction, stress distribution, and safety factors. Make iterative adjustments as needed. Finally, export your design for 3D printing or CNC machining.

The following timeline outlines a suggested project schedule to complete this hands-on exercise

Timeline and SMART Objectives

Week	Task	SMART Goal
1	Learn the Shape Generator and define project	Complete tutorial and sketch basic bracket shape in Inventor
2	Apply loads and constraints	Set up Shape Generator with correct boundary conditions by mid-week
3	Generate, simulate, and redesign bracket	Create three variations and test for stress and weight balance
4	Finalize and prepare for fabrication	Optimize model for 3D printing or CNC with complete documentation

This chapter has provided a thorough exploration of generative design as applied through Autodesk Inventor, highlighting how artificial intelligence is enabling engineers to move beyond conventional form-making into a world of data-driven design intelligence. From topology optimization to real-world aerospace and automotive applications, the integration of AI within Inventor allows professionals and learners alike to create lighter, stronger, and smarter components.

By engaging with the hands-on project, readers gain practical experience and unlock their ability to apply generative design principles to solve engineering challenges creatively and efficiently. As you proceed through this book, these foundational skills will serve as a stepping stone into more advanced AI integrations, including simulation, cloud collaboration, and automated design verification. The future of CAD is not just about drawing—it is about defining problems and letting AI deliver high-performance, manufacturable answers.

Chapter 3

AI-Driven 3D Modeling with SolidWorks

SolidWorks Xdesign is part of the 3DEXPERIENCE platform developed by Dassault Systèmes, representing a next-generation, cloud-based 3D modeling environment powered by artificial intelligence. Unlike traditional desktop versions of SolidWorks, Xdesign is designed from the ground up to leverage the power of AI, machine learning, and cloud computing for a more intelligent, responsive, and collaborative product design experience.

One of the core advantages of Xdesign lies in its ability to learn from user behavior and historical design data. The AI capabilities embedded within the software can analyze modeling patterns, anticipate design intent, and offer proactive suggestions. These capabilities are not just surface-level enhancements; they are deeply woven into the design pipeline, guiding everything from part creation to feature application, and even assembly configuration.

The cloud infrastructure of Xdesign ensures that users always have access to the most up-to-date tools and datasets, with no need for local installations or hardware constraints. This accessibility democratizes high-level design tools, making it easier for students, engineers, and professionals to create intelligent designs from anywhere, using any device with internet access.

Below is a conceptual diagram showing how AI operates within the Xdesign workflow

Diagram AI Workflow in SolidWorks Xdesign

Intelligent Part Recognition

One of the most innovative components of SolidWorks Xdesign is its machine learning-driven part recognition system. Traditional CAD tools require users to manually define and apply every modeling operation—whether it's an extrusion, hole, fillet, or rib. Xdesign, however, analyzes the geometry as it is built and uses prior knowledge from thousands of similar models to suggest optimal features in real time.

For example, when a user begins to draw a rectangular profile for a bracket, Xdesign's AI engine identifies the intent and preemptively suggests standard extrusion depths or hole placements based on past projects and industry standards. This feature is known as **Design**

Assistant, and it allows the software to streamline the modeling process by offering context-aware suggestions.

Furthermore, AI can also detect symmetry, suggest reuse of standard components, and recommend assembly mates that align with the designer's historical choices. The system becomes more intelligent the more it is used, adapting to the specific workflow and habits of the designer. This behavior is akin to a smart assistant that learns not only what to suggest but also when and how to deliver those suggestions without interrupting creative flow.

The following table illustrates typical AI-assisted feature recognition scenarios in Xdesign

Table   AI Feature Suggestion Examples in SolidWorks Xdesign

Modeling Context	AI Suggestion Type	Design Benefit
Extruding a basic 2D profile	Suggest optimal thickness and material	Saves time, ensures manufacturability
Drawing a hole pattern	Auto-array detection and pattern preview	Faster pattern creation, fewer clicks
Adding fillets on edges	Smart edge selection and	Ensures design consistency and

Modeling Context	AI Suggestion Type	Design Benefit
	radius guess	aesthetics
Assembling components	Auto-mating based on shape recognition	Eliminates tedious manual mating steps

Real-Time AI Collaboration in the Cloud

In addition to intelligent modeling, SolidWorks Xdesign introduces a groundbreaking AI-driven collaboration system. By operating fully in the cloud via the 3DEXPERIENCE platform, teams can work on the same model simultaneously, receive AI-based conflict alerts, and leverage smart version control powered by machine learning algorithms.

AI helps in resolving design conflicts when multiple users attempt to modify the same part. For instance, if one user changes a dimension while another adds a fillet, the AI evaluates the compatibility of both actions and provides real-time conflict resolution options, such as merging changes or selecting the most structurally viable option. This approach eliminates the traditional issues related to file locking, manual merging, or version mismatch.

Moreover, AI tracks the history of design decisions and offers contextual feedback based on team behavior. If a certain design variation caused issues in a previous iteration, the AI may flag it when a similar change is proposed. These intelligent interventions create a more resilient and efficient design environment.

From a project management perspective, Xdesign's AI capabilities extend to task prioritization, deadline prediction, and collaboration analytics. Teams can visualize who contributed to which feature, how often parts were revised, and where bottlenecks are occurring—all thanks to data-driven dashboards.

Designing an AI-Suggested Assembly Part

To fully understand and appreciate the AI-driven capabilities of SolidWorks Xdesign, readers are encouraged to complete a hands-on design project that involves creating a real-world mechanical assembly part with assistance from the software's intelligent tools.

Project Objective Create an assembly-ready connecting link, commonly used in robotic arms or hinge joints, with AI suggestions for feature placement, symmetry, and stress-based geometry refinement.

Step 1 Project Setup and Initial Sketch

Open a new project in SolidWorks Xdesign and begin by sketching a rectangular connecting body with two circular ends for fasteners. The Design Assistant will automatically suggest hole placements if symmetry is detected. Accept or adjust based on your requirements.

Step 2 Feature Enhancement via Design Assistant

Extrude the main profile and allow the AI engine to suggest depth based on typical material properties for aluminum. As you add holes or slots, notice how the assistant auto-completes patterns, saving you valuable time.

Use the AI-driven fillet tool to automatically select edges based on standard manufacturing radii. For further enhancement, apply chamfers on the contact surfaces where bolts will rest, and let Xdesign recommend common standards.

Step 3 Assembly and Mating

Load a prebuilt robotic base or bracket component into your cloud workspace. Drag the connecting link into the assembly view. The AI will propose mating constraints like concentric and coincident relationships based on geometry recognition. You can validate or override these suggestions.

After placement, use the real-time simulation tool to analyze stress points. The AI will detect underperforming areas and suggest reinforcement such as ribbing or material increase.

Step 4 Final Review and Export

Once the part is complete, share the design with collaborators. Use the AI version manager to view all changes made, and resolve any flagged conflicts. Export the model as a 3D printable STL file or prepare it for CNC machining.

The following timeline will help readers complete the project efficiently

Project Timeline and Milestones

Week	Task	SMART Goal
1	Launch Xdesign, sketch part base	Complete base sketch and receive initial AI suggestions
2	Add features and refine geometry	Apply extrusions, holes, and AI-recommended fillets
3	Assemble and simulate part	Mate components and validate structural behavior
4	Review version history and export design	Finalize the part and export for real-world fabrication or simulation

This chapter has explored how SolidWorks Xdesign integrates artificial intelligence into every layer of the design process—from part modeling to collaborative assemblies. By leveraging machine learning for feature recognition, geometry optimization, and cloud collaboration, Xdesign sets a new standard for CAD platforms.

The hands-on project provides practical experience with AI-suggested design flows, helping learners and professionals alike to adapt to modern engineering tools. As AI continues to evolve, the designers who embrace these technologies will be able to deliver faster, smarter, and more cost-effective solutions to real-world problems. In the next chapter, we will explore how AI can assist in simulation-driven design, ensuring that your models are not only intelligently built but also rigorously tested for real-world conditions using predictive analytics.

Chapter 4

Simulation & Analysis in Ansys Discovery

The evolution of simulation technology in engineering design has reached a significant milestone with the integration of artificial intelligence, particularly within platforms like **Ansys Discovery**. Traditionally, simulation required extensive computational time, complex meshing processes, and highly specialized expertise. However, the infusion of AI and machine learning into simulation tools has fundamentally changed how engineers approach product analysis, enabling **real-time, physics-based simulations** that are far more accessible and insightful.

Ansys Discovery is a next-generation simulation environment that blends the accuracy of high-fidelity solvers with the instant feedback of AI-powered computational guidance. AI algorithms in Discovery continuously learn from thousands of prior simulation cases and user interactions, allowing them to anticipate outcomes, highlight problem areas, and recommend adjustments even before a full-scale simulation is run. This predictive capability dramatically shortens the feedback loop, empowering designers to iterate faster and explore a broader range of design alternatives.

The platform uses **GPU acceleration** and neural network inference to enable on-the-fly simulations that would otherwise take hours using conventional finite element methods. In this sense, AI acts as a co-pilot in the simulation process—guiding engineers toward better designs by interpreting physical behavior with unprecedented speed.

To better visualize this integration, the following diagram outlines the flow of AI-enhanced simulation in Ansys Discovery

Diagram AI-Powered Simulation Workflow in Ansys Discovery

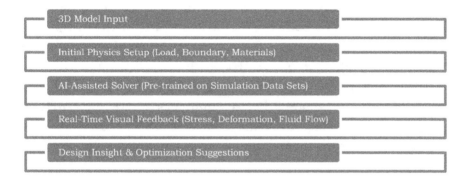

Stress Analysis and Performance Prediction

One of the most compelling applications of AI in Ansys Discovery is in the domain of **stress analysis and structural performance prediction**. Conventional simulation methods rely heavily on mesh refinement, solver configurations, and iterative post-processing. AI simplifies and accelerates this by offering **meshless simulation capabilities** or intelligently guiding mesh refinement where necessary, reducing computational cost without sacrificing accuracy.

When a user applies forces, loads, or constraints to a model in Discovery, AI algorithms interpret the boundary conditions and immediately provide color-mapped feedback showing areas of high stress concentration, possible failure points, and safety factors. This instant performance insight allows designers to identify critical flaws early in the process, long before prototypes are manufactured.

AI also helps predict **thermal behavior, fluid dynamics, and vibrational modes**, enabling a multi-physics analysis that would be otherwise too resource-intensive to conduct early in the design phase. By evaluating the sensitivity of parameters like material properties, geometry, and loading conditions, the system helps engineers make **data-driven decisions** on where to reinforce a structure, reduce weight, or change material selection.

A comparative table below shows how AI-enhanced stress analysis in Ansys Discovery compares with traditional simulation methods

Table Traditional vs AI-Enhanced Simulation Workflows

Simulation Task	Traditional Method	AI-Enhanced Method in Ansys Discovery
Meshing	Manual setup and refinement	AI suggests or bypasses complex

Simulation Task	Traditional Method	AI-Enhanced Method in Ansys Discovery
		meshing
Solver Time	Hours for complex simulations	Real-time feedback using AI-accelerated solvers
Interpretation of Results	Manual plotting and result review	AI auto-identifies critical stress zones
Design Adjustment	Separate redesign process	Instant feedback enables live model tweaking
Computational Resource Usage	CPU-intensive, often requires HPC	Efficient GPU usage with AI-optimized algorithms

AI and Material Optimization

Material selection is one of the most critical steps in any engineering design. The wrong choice can lead to premature failure, increased cost, or poor performance. Ansys Discovery integrates **machine learning models trained on vast material databases** to assist in this decision-making process.

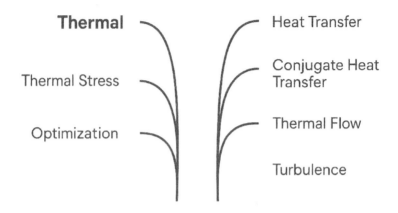

Thermal — Heat Transfer

Thermal Stress — Conjugate Heat Transfer

Optimization — Thermal Flow

Turbulence

SIMULATION & ANALYSIS

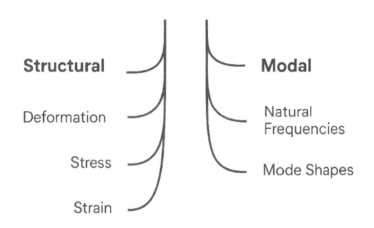

Structural — Modal

Deformation — Natural Frequencies

Stress — Mode Shapes

Strain

Figure 1 Components of Simulation with Ansys

These models analyze the geometry, expected loading, and operating conditions of a part, then propose materials that optimize strength-to-weight ratio, thermal resistance, fatigue life, and other properties.

What sets AI apart here is its ability to identify **non-obvious trade-offs**. For instance, while a traditional material selection approach might prioritize tensile strength alone, AI considers the interdependence of multiple criteria such as machinability, corrosion resistance, and cost-effectiveness. The result is a set of smart recommendations tailored to the specific simulation objectives.

Additionally, Ansys Discovery enables **automatic testing of multiple material scenarios** without requiring the user to restart the simulation each time. The AI engine cycles through material presets and displays the simulated behavior for each, helping users understand how performance varies and ensuring optimal selection with minimal guesswork.

The diagram below illustrates how AI facilitates material optimization

Diagram   AI-Assisted Material Selection and Testing

Simulating Load-Bearing Capacity

To bring all these AI-enhanced features into practical focus, let us walk through a hands-on simulation project using Ansys Discovery. This project involves creating and analyzing the **load-bearing capacity of a simple structural bracket**, commonly used in industrial machinery and automotive applications.

Project Setup

Start by modeling a flat bracket with two holes on either side, designed to be mounted onto a surface. The bracket features a central rib for added stiffness. Import this model into Ansys Discovery and initiate a structural simulation.

Physics Definition

Apply a fixed support boundary condition at the holes and a downward load on the bracket's center, simulating a weight-bearing application. The AI in Discovery automatically applies material properties based on initial selections or suggests alternatives from the internal database.

Simulation Execution

Upon clicking "Simulate," the system rapidly processes the load case and displays a real-time stress distribution plot. Areas of maximum stress appear in red, while zones of low stress remain blue. The AI assistant immediately flags overstressed regions and suggests modifying the geometry or selecting a higher-grade material.

Material Optimization

Activate the material recommendation engine. Ansys Discovery runs the same simulation across five material variants—aluminum 6061, stainless steel 304, titanium alloy, carbon fiber composite, and reinforced plastic. The AI provides a comparative matrix of each material's performance in terms of maximum displacement, stress, and safety factor.

Table Material Performance Summary for Bracket Simulation

Material	Max Stress (MPa)	Max Displacement (mm)	Safety Factor	Weight (grams)
Aluminum 6061	145	1.2	2.5	210
Stainless Steel 304	120	0.9	3.1	360
Titanium Alloy	98	0.6	4.0	185
Carbon Fiber Composite	130	1.0	2.8	110
Reinforced Plastic	175	2.0	1.9	90

Based on performance and weight goals, the AI recommends titanium alloy for high strength and low weight, or carbon fiber if cost constraints are significant. The user can then finalize the design and export it for 3D printing, CNC machining, or further optimization. Ansys Discovery exemplifies the future of simulation in engineering—**instantaneous, intelligent, and intuitive**. By combining AI with physics-based solvers, engineers can explore more design possibilities in less time and with greater confidence. The platform's ability to predict stress behavior, evaluate performance, and recommend optimal materials allows teams to transition from conceptualization to production faster and more effectively than ever before. This chapter provided a comprehensive look at how AI is revolutionizing simulation workflows through real-time physics guidance, intelligent stress detection, and machine learning-driven material selection. With hands-on experience, users can witness firsthand the transformative power of AI in simulation.

Chapter 5

AI-Driven 3D Scanning & Reverse Engineering with Geomagic Design X

Reverse engineering has always been a critical process in engineering, manufacturing, and product design. It involves recreating a digital model of an existing physical object to analyze, improve, reproduce, or modify it. Traditional reverse engineering relies heavily on manual modeling, extensive time investment, and expert-level CAD knowledge. However, the integration of **artificial intelligence (AI)** into tools like **Geomagic Design X** has transformed this field into a highly automated and intelligent process.

AI plays a pivotal role in interpreting raw 3D scan data and automatically identifying geometric features such as holes, fillets, chamfers, planes, and curves. These features, once recognized, are quickly and accurately reconstructed into a parametric CAD model that reflects the original physical object's dimensions and tolerances. What used to take days or even weeks can now be accomplished in hours, with higher accuracy and repeatability.

AI also helps resolve common challenges in reverse engineering, such as incomplete scan data, noise, and misalignment. Using trained neural networks, the system can infer missing surfaces, repair scan errors, and align parts precisely, even when the original object is asymmetrical or complex.

This entire process can be visualized in the following diagram

Diagram AI Workflow in Reverse Engineering

3D Scanning of Physical Object

Importing Point Cloud or Mesh into Geomagic Design X

AI-Powered Feature Recognition and Segmentation

Automatic Surface and Solid Reconstruction

Parametric CAD Model Generation

Mesh-to-CAD Conversion with Machine Learning

One of the most labor-intensive aspects of reverse engineering is converting **mesh data into precise CAD geometry**. Meshes are made up of thousands to millions of small triangles (also called facets), which are good for rendering but difficult to use for design or manufacturing. Engineers need solid bodies with parametric features that can be edited, dimensioned, and reused. This is where **machine learning algorithms** come into play.

Geomagic Design X employs deep learning techniques trained on vast libraries of mechanical parts and organic shapes. These algorithms classify regions of the mesh and recommend the most likely geometric features. For example, a circular hole in a mesh will be automatically recognized as a feature that can be converted into a parametric cylinder with specific diameter and depth. Planar faces, revolved features, and symmetric patterns are also intelligently identified and labeled.

The advantage here is not just speed, but **accuracy and design intent recognition**. AI is capable of interpreting not just what the geometry is, but why it exists, helping recreate models that align closely with engineering standards. Machine learning also learns from user corrections. If a feature is misidentified, the user's correction is noted, improving future predictions.

To show how this AI-driven conversion compares with traditional manual techniques, the table below offers a performance breakdown

Table   Mesh-to-CAD Conversion – Manual vs AI-Driven Workflow

Feature	Manual Workflow	AI-Driven Workflow in Geomagic Design X
Feature Detection Time	Several hours per part	Real-time or under 10 minutes
Accuracy	Depends on user skill	High consistency with geometric inference

Feature	Manual Workflow	AI-Driven Workflow in Geomagic Design X
Editable CAD Model Output	Requires rework	Fully parametric and editable in SolidWorks, NX, etc.
Recognition of Design Intent	Manual approximation	AI-powered logic-based feature detection
Learning Over Time	None	Continuously improves with user feedback

AI in Point Cloud Processing

Point clouds are raw sets of spatial data points collected during 3D scanning. A high-resolution scan can produce **millions of points**, and processing them efficiently is crucial for a successful reverse engineering workflow. Without AI, users would need to manually clean noise, align scans, merge point clouds, and remove redundant data. This process can be complex and overwhelming, especially when dealing with intricate or partially damaged objects.

With AI-enhanced point cloud processing in Geomagic Design X, users experience a **smarter workflow**. AI algorithms filter out noise by identifying outlier points that do not conform to expected geometry. For instance, a scratch or dirt on the object's surface might distort the point cloud—but AI can recognize and remove such anomalies, preserving the accuracy of the model.

AI also assists in **automatic alignment of multiple scans**, especially when parts of the object have been captured from different angles.

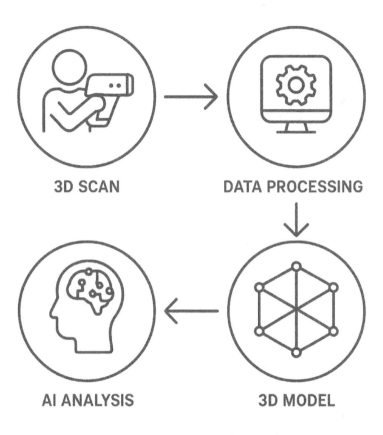

3D SCAN   DATA PROCESSING

AI ANALYSIS   3D MODEL

Instead of relying solely on manual reference points, the software identifies overlapping regions and matches them using intelligent pattern recognition, ensuring that the final point cloud is cohesive and accurate.

Additionally, AI can fill missing data by extrapolating from surrounding geometry. For example, if part of a circular edge is missing, the system can recreate the curve based on the rest of the data. This enables reverse engineering even when the object is partially damaged or difficult to scan.

The following diagram illustrates the AI-enhanced point cloud processing steps

Diagram AI-Powered Point Cloud Refinement

Creating a CAD Model from a 3D Scan

To fully understand how AI enhances reverse engineering in a practical context, let's walk through a project where we create a **fully parametric CAD model from a 3D scan** of an existing mechanical component—a simple gear housing.

Step 1 3D Scanning

Begin by scanning the object using a handheld 3D scanner, such as the Artec Eva or Creaform HandySCAN. The scan captures high-resolution data of the gear housing from multiple angles. The raw point cloud is then exported in formats like .PLY or .STL and imported into Geomagic Design X.

Step 2 AI-Enhanced Cleanup

Once inside Geomagic Design X, initiate the **point cloud processing** module. The AI automatically filters noise, removes floating artifacts, and aligns scan sets using intelligent feature matching. The point cloud is then converted into a watertight mesh using automatic surface fitting.

Step 3 Feature Recognition and Modeling

Next, activate the **AI-powered mesh-to-CAD module**. The software begins analyzing the mesh and recognizing features such as cylindrical bosses, bolt holes, flat mounting surfaces, and inner cavities. It automatically recreates these as parametric CAD features.

Step 4 Editing and Export

With the parametric model created, users can adjust dimensions, apply constraints, and prepare the file for further editing in SolidWorks, Siemens NX, or Autodesk

Inventor. The model is fully editable, and all features are stored in a CAD history tree.

To illustrate the transformation, the following table compares key stages of the model development process

Table Project Timeline – Gear Housing Reverse Engineering

Stage	Time Taken	AI Features Involved	Output Format
3D Scanning	10 minutes	None	Raw Point Cloud (.PLY)
AI Point Cloud Cleanup	5 minutes	Noise Filtering, Alignment	Clean Mesh (.STL)
Feature Recognition & Modeling	15 minutes	Cylinder/Plane/Fillet Detection	Parametric Model
CAD Export & Adjustment	5 minutes	Design Tree Generation	.SLDPRT or .STEP

This chapter highlights the revolutionary impact of artificial intelligence in the realm of 3D scanning and reverse engineering. Geomagic Design X exemplifies how AI can drastically simplify, accelerate, and improve the accuracy of the reverse engineering process. Whether you're digitizing legacy parts, replicating damaged equipment, or creating parametric models for simulation and redesign, the power of AI transforms a traditionally complex workflow into an efficient and intelligent experience.

Chapter 6

AI-Powered Lattice Structures

Lattice structures are intricate internal geometries that consist of repeating unit cells arranged in a pattern to provide strength, stiffness, and thermal properties while significantly reducing weight. These structures are not just aesthetically unique but functionally powerful, especially when applied to additive manufacturing. With conventional CAD tools, designing such geometries is often time-consuming, manually intensive, and limited in complexity. This is where **nTopology**, an advanced engineering design software, leverages **artificial intelligence (AI)** and field-driven design to automate and optimize lattice generation in ways that are mathematically precise and practically manufacturable.

AI-powered design engines within nTopology analyze part geometry, loading conditions, and user-defined constraints to automatically generate lattice patterns tailored to specific performance goals. These goals can range from weight reduction and strength-to-weight ratio maximization to vibration damping or heat dissipation. Instead of relying on manual input, AI algorithms model the interaction between loads and internal structures, dynamically varying the lattice size, thickness, and orientation based on stress gradients or deformation regions.

The result is an intelligent generation of functionally graded lattice structures that are optimized not only for performance but also for manufacturability using modern 3D printing techniques. The entire process—powered by field-driven design and algorithmic modeling—goes beyond traditional parametric CAD tools, enabling engineers to create forms once considered impossible.

Diagram   AI-Driven Lattice Design Workflow in nTopology

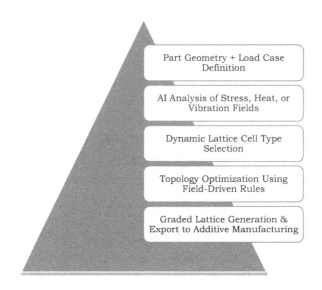

Part Geometry + Load Case Definition

AI Analysis of Stress, Heat, or Vibration Fields

Dynamic Lattice Cell Type Selection

Topology Optimization Using Field-Driven Rules

Graded Lattice Generation & Export to Additive Manufacturing

Lightweight Engineering & Manufacturing

One of the primary goals of incorporating lattice structures into engineering design is **lightweighting**, which is the reduction of mass without compromising the part's functionality or integrity. Lightweight engineering plays a critical role in industries such as aerospace, automotive, and medical devices, where every gram saved translates into improved fuel efficiency, payload capacity, or patient comfort.

In nTopology, AI allows designers to define field parameters—such as von Mises stress, displacement fields, or even multi-physics criteria like thermal expansion—and use these parameters to drive the variation of lattice density or wall thickness. This dynamic control means that materials are used only where needed, allowing for optimized material distribution that is **highly efficient** and **tailored to real-world conditions**.

Additive manufacturing, particularly Selective Laser Sintering (SLS), Direct Metal Laser Sintering (DMLS), and Fused Deposition Modeling (FDM), complements this design approach by enabling the fabrication of these highly complex lattice geometries. Traditional manufacturing methods cannot easily replicate such intricate structures due to tooling limitations. AI, paired with additive manufacturing, unleashes new design freedoms, where internal cavities, generative trusses, and cellular structures can be printed without human intervention.

To better understand the implications, consider the comparison in the following table

Table   Conventional vs AI-Driven Lightweight Design

Parameter	Conventional Design	AI-Powered Lattice Design in nTopology
Weight Reduction Potential	10–20%	30–70%

Parameter	Conventional Design	AI-Powered Lattice Design in nTopology
Structural Complexity	Simple shapes	Functionally graded lattices
Design Time	High	Reduced via automation
Performance Customization	Limited	Tuned to local stresses
Compatibility with 3D Printing	Moderate	Fully compatible
Material Efficiency	Moderate	High (only used where needed)

Performance Gains in 3D-Printed Parts

AI-generated lattice structures are not just about making parts lighter—they also lead to **tangible performance improvements**. These improvements can manifest in various ways, depending on the type of application and the design objectives set during the optimization process. In aerospace applications, AI-designed brackets and mounts with lattice cores can absorb vibrations and mechanical loads better than solid counterparts while significantly reducing overall part mass. This not only reduces fuel consumption but also extends component life due to enhanced stress distribution. In biomedical implants, such as orthopedic bone scaffolds, lattice structures are used to mimic the porous nature of natural bone. AI can optimize pore size and connectivity to ensure tissue integration and nutrient flow, improving patient recovery and implant success. For consumer products and sports equipment, AI-driven lattice geometries offer shock absorption, flexibility, and ergonomic shaping that would be impossible to achieve manually. Shoes with 3D-printed lattice midsoles, for example, provide a combination of cushioning and energy return tailored to the user's gait.

3D-Printed Lattice-Based Component

Let's explore a practical example to consolidate the concepts of AI-enhanced lattice generation and lightweighting using nTopology. The goal of this project is to design a **lattice-based load-bearing bracket** that is optimized for strength, weight, and manufacturability using metal additive manufacturing.

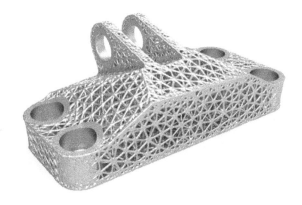

Step 1 Define the Bracket Geometry and Load Case

Begin by importing or sketching a simple bracket model that connects two mechanical assemblies. Define the boundary conditions, including fixed holes and regions where load is applied (e.g., 1000 N along a bolt axis).

Step 2 Apply Field-Driven Design Parameters

Using nTopology's simulation fields, apply a stress field across the bracket body. The software will generate a heatmap showing areas of high and low mechanical stress. Define rules such that areas with high stress get denser lattice structures, while low-stress zones get more open lattices.

Step 3 AI-Driven Lattice Creation

Choose a unit cell (e.g., gyroid, diamond, or octet) and allow the AI algorithms to generate a volumetric lattice structure within the bracket's solid body. The lattice will be automatically varied in density and size based on the previously calculated field parameters.

Step 4 Validate and Optimize

Run a lightweight topology optimization routine with AI assistance to fine-tune the lattice, ensuring the bracket meets stiffness and displacement requirements while minimizing material usage.

Step 5 Prepare for 3D Printing

Export the model as an STL or 3MF file. You can then slice it using metal AM-compatible software such as EOSPRINT or Renishaw's QuantAM. The final part can be printed using titanium alloy (Ti6Al4V), ensuring high strength and corrosion resistance. The timeline and performance metrics for this project are summarized in the table below

Table   Project   Overview   –   AI-Optimized Lattice Bracket

Stage	Time Required	AI Features Used	Outcome
Geometry & Load Setup	20 minutes	Field Mapping	Bracket Base + Load Field
Lattice Generation	30 minutes	Dynamic Unit Cell Sizing	Graded Internal Structure
Optimization & Simulation	45 minutes	Topology Optimization, AI Solver	Max Strength / Min Weight
3D Print Preparation	15 minutes	File Clean-Up	STL / 3MF File for DMLS
Final Weight Reduction Achieved	—	—	65% Reduction vs Solid Model

AI-powered lattice structure design in nTopology is a revolution in engineering optimization and advanced manufacturing. By merging algorithmic logic, real-time simulation data, and machine learning algorithms, engineers now have the tools to build components that are not only structurally efficient but also incredibly lightweight and ready for complex additive manufacturing workflows. This chapter has demonstrated how AI is redefining what's possible in engineering design, offering new dimensions of creativity and performance. The practical project further equips readers with the knowledge and confidence to start implementing AI-enhanced lattice design in their own workflows.

Chapter 7

Rendering & Visualization with KeyShot AI

In the domain of digital design visualization, achieving photorealism has always been a benchmark for success. Whether showcasing a new consumer product or validating the aesthetics of a mechanical part, realistic rendering plays a crucial role in communicating intent and attracting stakeholder approval. KeyShot, a leading software in the rendering ecosystem, has integrated artificial intelligence (AI) to significantly improve both the **efficiency** and **quality** of rendering workflows.

Traditional rendering processes require manual tuning of numerous parameters, such as material types, reflection indices, roughness, subsurface scattering, and lighting angle. These variables interact in complex ways, and only experienced professionals could traditionally produce truly realistic outputs. However, with the integration of AI into KeyShot, the software now offers **intelligent automation** of these visual decisions by analyzing image content, environment, and part geometry to automatically determine optimal rendering settings.

AI algorithms in KeyShot assist in real-time adjustments of textures and material surfaces based on physical simulation data. For instance, when rendering metallic surfaces, AI predicts how micro-scratches, oxidation layers, and ambient reflections should interact based on the type of alloy and surrounding lighting. This is no longer a matter of guesswork or complex shader tweaking—it is automated, contextual, and incredibly precise.

To appreciate this transformation, we can examine a simplified table comparing traditional and AI-assisted workflows for rendering a product made of composite materials under a softbox lighting environment.

Table   Traditional vs AI-Assisted Material Rendering in KeyShot

Rendering Step	Traditional Workflow	AI-Assisted KeyShot Workflow
Material Assignment	Manual selection and tuning	Auto-detection based on geometry
Light Bouncing Simulation	Ray bounces require trial & error	AI predicts accurate lighting curves
Reflection and Refraction	Manually adjusted shader settings	AI simulates physical material rules
Texture Mapping	Hand-placement or UV mapping	AI aligns textures using smart wrap
Result Accuracy	Depends on expertise	Uniformly high with fewer inputs

AI-Based IBL and Scene Setup

One of the most groundbreaking uses of AI in KeyShot is in **image-based lighting (IBL)**. This approach involves illuminating a 3D object using a high-dynamic-range image

(HDRI) that mimics real-world lighting environments. Traditionally, designers needed to import HDRI maps manually, adjust the scene orientation, fine-tune exposure, and align the environment to suit the product. This process, while powerful, was cumbersome and prone to inconsistencies.

KeyShot AI dramatically simplifies this task. Upon loading a model, the software analyzes the object's geometry, dimensions, and context, then suggests optimal IBL environments from its library. The AI can even generate a custom HDRI based on user-provided product descriptions or images, effectively reverse-engineering a plausible lighting scene that enhances realism.

Moreover, automated scene setup is no longer limited to lighting alone. AI in KeyShot evaluates camera angles, focal lengths, and even depth-of-field blur to compose the scene just like a professional photographer would. The system intelligently avoids visual clutter, unintentional occlusions, and awkward perspectives. It ensures the product is showcased with ideal framing, highlighting textures, contours, and color contrasts with cinematic precision.

This integration of AI not only reduces time but also ensures that every visualization reaches a professional standard, even if the user lacks experience in composition or lighting theory.

Rapid Iteration and Visualization

One of the greatest advantages of AI integration into rendering workflows is the acceleration of **design iteration cycles**. Previously, a single rendering could take minutes to hours, depending on the resolution and complexity. Designers would tweak material or lighting, wait for the results, and then repeat—often iterating dozens of times before achieving a satisfactory image.

With AI in KeyShot, rendering iterations are now **quasi-instantaneous**. The AI engine uses deep learning-based denoising and predictive path tracing to generate clean, high-resolution outputs from low-sample renders. Instead of rendering an entire scene with millions of rays, AI fills in the missing data with astonishing accuracy, allowing users to preview near-final results in seconds.

This speed allows for **real-time design validation**, where designers, engineers, or marketing teams can adjust colors, finishes, or backgrounds during live review sessions. The implications are significant product development cycles are shortened, client feedback loops are accelerated, and creative exploration is no longer bottlenecked by rendering delays. The following table summarizes how AI boosts iterative visualization performance

Table   Design Iteration Speed Improvement with AI

Activity	Traditional Time (mins)	AI-Assisted Time (mins)	Improvement
Material Update & Preview	10	1	10× Faster
Lighting Reconfiguration	15	1	15× Faster
Camera Repositioning & Refocus	5	0.5	10× Faster
High-Res Render (Final Output)	60	5	12× Faster

Rendering a Photorealistic Product

To bring all the above concepts to life, let us walk through a hands-on project using KeyShot AI **creating a photorealistic rendering of a wearable smartwatch prototype**. This product includes a metallic bezel, rubberized strap, touch-sensitive glass, and a colored LED display.

Step 1 Model Import

Begin by importing the 3D model of the smartwatch in a format such as .OBJ or .STEP. KeyShot AI will auto-detect materials and part types, grouping similar surfaces together.

Step 2 Material AI Mapping

Select "AI Smart Material Mode." The system will automatically assign appropriate materials based on geometry and part labels. The bezel will receive a brushed stainless steel finish, the strap a silicone rubber texture, and the screen a glossy transparent glass shader.

Step 3 Environment & Lighting

Use KeyShot's AI-assisted IBL feature. Upload a lifestyle photo of a wrist or outdoor scene, and KeyShot will generate a matching HDRI map, accurately reflecting light and color tones suitable for a smartwatch product shoot.

Step 4 Scene Composition

Activate the Auto-Framing and Smart Depth-of-Field tools. The AI will rotate, zoom, and tilt the camera to highlight the watch face while slightly blurring the strap and background to draw visual focus.

Step 5 Rendering

Click "AI Denoised Render." The software will process an 8K output with predictive noise reduction, smart light bloom, and realistic surface reflections—all in under five minutes.

Here is a summary table of the project phases

Table Smartwatch Rendering with KeyShot AI

Step	Task Description	AI Feature Used	Time Required
Model Import	Load and parse smartwatch CAD	Auto-material detection	2 minutes
Material Application	Apply realistic textures and surface types	Smart Material Assignment	3 minutes
Lighting Environment	Generate natural lighting for product feel	AI-Generated HDRI	2 minutes
Camera & Focus Setup	Auto-position camera and set depth-of-field	Auto Scene Composition	1 minute
Rendering & Export	Produce 8K photorealistic image	AI Denoising + Adaptive Sampling	5 minutes

AI integration within KeyShot has fundamentally transformed how designers, engineers, and marketers approach product visualization. What once required a high level of artistic skill and technical expertise is now accessible to a broader audience. Through intelligent lighting suggestions, realistic material prediction, automated scene setup, and real-time denoising, AI ensures that every render not only looks professional but also gets completed in a fraction of the traditional time.

This chapter explored the depth and capabilities of AI in KeyShot, making it clear that the future of rendering is not just visual—it is intelligent, iterative, and immersive. In the following chapter, we will explore how these AI-rendered visuals can be seamlessly integrated into immersive AR/VR experiences to close the loop between design and user experience.

Chapter 8

Toolpath Generation in Fusion 360 CAM

In the world of modern manufacturing, the integration of artificial intelligence into computer-aided manufacturing (CAM) software has marked a transformative leap forward. Fusion 360 CAM, developed by Autodesk, has taken center stage by embedding AI algorithms into its machining workflow to help users generate efficient, accurate, and intelligent toolpaths for CNC operations. Traditionally, generating a CNC toolpath involved selecting a series of machining operations such as facing, contouring, pocketing, and drilling. Each operation required manual input of speeds, feeds, tool engagement strategies, and sequence planning.

With AI integration, Fusion 360 now analyzes part geometry, tool availability, machine capabilities, and material properties to suggest and generate optimal toolpaths. This dramatically reduces trial-and-error, which often consumes time, resources, and materials. AI systems in Fusion 360 CAM can automatically choose the best entry and exit points, calculate optimal step-down and step-over parameters, and even adapt to machine-specific constraints such as spindle speed limitations and travel ranges. These AI-generated toolpaths are not only more efficient but also safer for the tooling and the machine, minimizing wear and potential collisions.

One of the key concepts introduced by AI in CAM is the **use of predictive analytics**. By examining thousands of machining jobs—either from past user data or cloud-based datasets—AI systems can predict the most effective strategies for any given geometry and suggest operation sequences that reduce tool retraction, repositioning, and air cutting. This leads to tighter cycle times and higher quality surface finishes.

Table Comparison of Manual vs AI-Optimized Toolpath Generation

Feature	Traditional CAM (Manual)	AI-Optimized CAM in Fusion 360
Toolpath Strategy Selection	Based on user experience	Data-driven decision-making
Tool Engagement	Manual entry of step-over/depth	AI-calculated dynamic engagement
Entry/Exit Paths	Fixed or simple ramp/plunge	AI-adapted for geometry and tooling
Cycle Time Optimization	User-iterated	Auto-optimized with simulations
Collision Avoidance	Set manually or with limited checks	Real-time adaptive avoidance

AI in Material Removal Simulation

A critical component of the CAM process is material removal simulation. In Fusion 360, AI augments this simulation by using machine learning models that predict how materials behave during milling, turning, or drilling. These simulations traditionally required high computational resources and often depended on simplified physics engines. With AI, the system leverages previously computed scenarios and advanced physics-based simulations to generate fast, yet accurate representations of the machining process.

AI-enhanced material removal simulation can provide real-time feedback on machining efficiency. For instance, it can highlight areas where the tool is underutilized or overstressed. By analyzing these insights, Fusion 360 CAM automatically modifies the toolpath to achieve better tool wear distribution and improved surface quality. This feedback loop, driven by AI, enables the software to fine-tune cutting parameters dynamically, not only for one operation but across the entire sequence.

Additionally, material removal AI now includes **thermal and force modeling**. It can estimate hotspots and predict excessive tool loading, which often causes breakage or deflection. Based on these predictions, Fusion 360 CAM adjusts feed rates and spindle speeds on the fly. This level of predictive simulation elevates the safety and precision of CNC operations, especially in aerospace and medical applications where micrometer-level tolerance is critical.

Machine Learning in Adaptive Machining

Adaptive machining refers to the real-time alteration of machining strategies based on changing conditions during manufacturing. Fusion 360 CAM incorporates machine learning (ML) techniques to evolve these adaptive strategies based on user behavior, machining history, and process feedback. The software becomes smarter over time, learning from previous machining operations to offer context-aware recommendations.

For example, when working with titanium or Inconel, the software might initially suggest a conservative approach due to the materials' tough nature. But over several runs, it learns how the user's machine responds to higher spindle loads or deeper cuts and starts adjusting accordingly. This machine learning mechanism adapts toolpaths in future operations, optimizing for individual shop floor environments.

Another important aspect of adaptive machining is **re-machining detection**. After initial roughing, the AI identifies leftover stock and automatically applies finishing or rest-machining toolpaths only where needed. This intelligent feature minimizes redundant cuts and dramatically speeds up the process. Moreover, if the geometry is modified after initial toolpath generation—common during prototype revisions—the AI adjusts toolpaths without requiring a complete reprogramming session.

Table   Fusion 360 Adaptive Machining Features Enhanced by Machine Learning

Feature	Description	ML Enhancement
Rest Machining	Removes remaining material in corners/deep areas	Learns from geometry and previous cycles
Tool Wear Compensation	Adapts feeds/speeds based on wear history	Predicts tool degradation from past runs
Feature Recognition	Identifies pockets, slots, bosses	Learns user preferences over time
Tool Library Selection	Suggests suitable tools	Personalizes tool choices by job type

CNC Toolpath Optimization

Let's now dive into a practical hands-on example to apply these AI-powered capabilities in Fusion 360 CAM. The project involves generating toolpaths for a **prototype drone motor mount** made from aluminum 6061. The mount features multiple pockets, countersunk holes, and tight tolerances around the shaft bearing area.

Step 1 Import the CAD Model

Load the motor mount's 3D model into Fusion 360. Once imported, select the **Manufacture Workspace** and initiate a new setup. AI will automatically detect the part's bounding box and suggest a coordinate system aligned to the top face.

Step 2 Material and Machine Configuration

Choose Aluminum 6061 as the workpiece material. The AI will use this data to inform speeds, feeds, and chip load estimates. Next, define the machine tool—a 3-axis CNC router with a max spindle speed of 12,000 RPM.

Step 3 Operation Selection

Let Fusion 360 suggest toolpaths using its AI recommendation engine. For this project, it may choose 2D Adaptive Clearing for roughing, followed by 2D Contour for finishing, and a Circular Bore operation for countersinking.

Step 4 Toolpath Simulation

Run the AI-enhanced material removal simulation. The software will display heat zones, force vectors on the endmill, and predicted surface finish. If hotspots or over-engagement areas appear, adjust the strategy or let AI auto-optimize.

Step 5 Post-Processing

Once satisfied, use Fusion 360's post-processing engine to generate G-code for your specific CNC controller (e.g., GRBL, Fanuc, Mach3). Review the optimized toolpaths and simulate the motion in your CNC machine's software for validation.

Table   AI-Optimized   Toolpath   Project Summary

Step	Task Description	AI Feature Used	Time Saved
Setup Configuration	Auto-coordinate detection	Smart Setup Assistant	5 mins
Operation Planning	Suggested toolpaths for part geometry	AI Operation Planner	20 mins
Simulation	Visual feedback + heat prediction	Real-Time Physics & ML	30 mins
Optimization	Auto-adjust feeds/stepover	Adaptive Toolpath Engine	25 mins
Post-Processing	Machine-specific G-code generation	AI G-code Mapping	10 mins

Fusion 360 CAM's integration of AI and machine learning technologies represents a fundamental evolution in how

digital fabrication is approached. By combining toolpath intelligence, material behavior prediction, and adaptive learning, the software enables manufacturers, engineers, and even small makers to achieve industrial-level efficiency and precision without the traditional overhead of manual programming. The impact of these AI features is clear—not only are jobs completed faster, but the quality and consistency of the machined parts are vastly improved. This chapter has guided readers through both the conceptual foundation and practical application of AI-enhanced CAM, setting the stage for even more advanced integrations in future chapters.

Chapter 9

Automated 3D Printing with Autodesk Netfabb

The advent of artificial intelligence in additive manufacturing has introduced a significant evolution in the 3D printing industry. Autodesk Netfabb, a powerful software solution for additive manufacturing, has integrated AI tools that automate several critical aspects of the 3D printing workflow, from support structure generation to defect detection, and even optimization for multi-material printing. By leveraging AI, Netfabb transforms how engineers and manufacturers prepare and optimize 3D models for printing, streamlining production and improving efficiency.

In traditional 3D printing workflows, tasks like designing support structures, detecting potential defects, or optimizing the slicing process were often tedious, time-consuming, and required expertise. However, with AI-powered features in Autodesk Netfabb, these processes are automated, reducing the manual effort required and ensuring better-quality prints. The role of AI is particularly important in ensuring the print quality of complex geometries, reducing material waste, and improving the overall speed of the printing process.

AI-Powered Support Structure Generation

One of the most challenging aspects of additive manufacturing is the generation of support structures for overhanging or complex geometries. Support structures are necessary to provide stability during the printing process, but they often increase material consumption and require post-processing for removal. Historically, designing these structures manually involved careful calculations to ensure that they were strong enough to support the printed part while minimizing material use and complexity.

Autodesk Netfabb utilizes AI-powered algorithms to automatically generate optimized support structures. These algorithms analyze the geometry of the part and determine the most efficient and effective configuration of supports. The AI considers factors like the part's orientation, weight distribution, overhangs, and the printing material's properties. As a result, Netfabb produces support structures that not only ensure a successful print but also minimize the amount of support material required, which in turn reduces waste and costs.

AI enhances the process by iterating through numerous design options quickly, offering support designs that human designers might overlook. Furthermore, it allows for adaptive support generation, which adjusts in real-time as the design evolves. This intelligent system also has the capacity to suggest the optimal orientation for printing the part, which can lead to improved mechanical properties and printability, particularly when working with complex or high-performance materials.

Table   AI-Powered Support Structure vs. Manual Support Design

Feature	Traditional Manual Design	AI-Powered Support Generation
Support	Manually designed	AI automates

Feature	Traditional Manual Design	AI-Powered Support Generation
Structure Creation	based on experience and trial-and-error	generation based on part geometry
Material Efficiency	Requires adjustments to minimize waste	Optimizes support material usage
Print Time and Cost	Higher due to inefficient design	Reduced print time and material costs
Complexity Handling	Difficult for complex geometries	Automatically adapts to complex designs
Post-Processing	Often requires labor-intensive removal of supports	Minimizes the need for post-processing

Automated Defect Detection

Another groundbreaking application of AI in Autodesk Netfabb is automated defect detection. In traditional additive manufacturing, detecting defects such as layer misalignment, warping, or internal voids was a manual and labor-intensive process. Often, it required significant post-print inspection and testing to identify and correct issues. With AI, Netfabb has incorporated defect detection into the design phase, using machine learning algorithms to predict potential print failures.

These AI algorithms examine the 3D model for common issues such as thin walls, improper wall thickness, or unsupported areas that might lead to failure during printing. The system can also detect anomalies in the printing path or slicing process, predicting areas of the part that may be prone to thermal stresses or warping. If potential issues are identified, the software provides suggestions on how to adjust the part design, print settings, or orientation to mitigate the risks.

The AI also continuously learns from the success or failure of previous prints, improving its defect detection capabilities over time. For example, if a part repeatedly experiences warping in certain conditions, the system will identify this pattern and proactively suggest corrective actions for future prints.

AI-Assisted Slicing for 3D Printing

Multi-material 3D printing adds another layer of complexity to the design and printing process. In multi-material prints, different materials are used in specific regions of the part to optimize functionality, such as combining rigid and flexible materials in one object. However, the challenge lies in managing the transitions between materials, ensuring good bonding between them, and optimizing printing parameters for each material type.

In Autodesk Netfabb, AI assists with the slicing process for multi-material 3D printing by automatically generating the most efficient slicing strategy based on the properties of the materials used. The AI system considers factors such as material compatibility, thermal behavior, and layer bonding to optimize the slicing parameters for each material zone. It also suggests the best way to print the material interfaces, ensuring that the transition between materials is smooth, without compromising the strength or integrity of the part.

The AI can also dynamically adjust print settings like temperature, extrusion speed, and layer height depending on the material type in each section. This ensures that the final printed part meets both functional and aesthetic requirements, while minimizing the chance of defects such as delamination or poor adhesion between materials.

Table   Traditional vs. AI-Assisted Slicing for Multi-Material Printing

Aspect	Traditional Slicing	AI-Assisted Slicing
Material Transition Handling	Manual adjustment of settings	AI automatically optimizes material transitions
Print Setting Adjustment	Requires manual input for each material	Dynamic adjustments based on material behavior
Defect Detection	No real-time defect	Predicts potential issues like

Aspect	Traditional Slicing	AI-Assisted Slicing
	prediction	delamination
Print Time Optimization	Time-consuming trial and error	Optimized for quicker, more efficient prints

3D Printing of a Complex Part

Let's now explore a hands-on project where AI optimization can be applied to a complex part for 3D printing. For this project, we will design a **heat sink for a high-performance electronic component** that requires both lightweight properties and excellent thermal conductivity. The part will use two materials a rigid, thermally conductive material for the body and a flexible, heat-resistant material for the support structure.

Step 1 Import and Prepare the 3D Model

Begin by importing the heat sink design into Autodesk Netfabb. The AI will automatically detect key features like the channels for heat dissipation and the overhangs that will require support.

Step 2 AI-Powered Support Generation

Let the AI generate the most efficient support structure. It will consider the part's orientation and geometry to create supports that minimize material use and ensure that the part will not experience warping during the print. The AI system will also suggest the best orientation for printing to avoid unnecessary support material.

Step 3 Automated Defect Detection

The AI system scans the model and identifies potential issues. For example, it might detect that certain areas of the part are too thin, potentially leading to weak points. The system suggests increasing the thickness of certain regions to improve the structural integrity of the heat sink without affecting the overall design.

Step 4 Slicing for Multi-Material Printing

The next step is slicing the part for multi-material printing. Autodesk Netfabb's AI system automatically identifies the regions of the part that will use the rigid, thermally conductive material and those that will use the flexible support material. It adjusts the slicing parameters for each material type, ensuring smooth transitions between materials and optimizing print settings to avoid delamination.

Step 5 3D Print and Evaluation

Finally, generate the G-code for your 3D printer. Once the part is printed, evaluate the results by checking the quality of the support structure, surface finish, and overall print accuracy. The AI-optimized approach ensures that the part meets the required specifications without wasting material.

Autodesk Netfabb's integration of AI into the 3D printing workflow provides an enormous boost to efficiency, quality, and precision in additive manufacturing. AI-driven support generation, defect detection, and multi-material slicing offer not only convenience but also enable the creation of more complex, high-performance parts that were previously difficult or even impossible to produce with traditional methods. As additive manufacturing continues to evolve, AI will undoubtedly play a central role in shaping the future of 3D printing by making it smarter, faster, and more sustainable. This chapter has equipped you with the tools and knowledge to start applying AI to your 3D printing processes, enhancing your ability to produce high-quality, optimized parts.

Chapter 10

AR & VR in CAD with NVIDIA Omniverse

In recent years, the integration of Artificial Intelligence (AI) with Augmented Reality (AR) and Virtual Reality (VR) has revolutionized the way engineers, designers, and manufacturers interact with Computer-Aided Design (CAD) models. Traditionally, CAD models were restricted to flat, two-dimensional screens, limiting users' ability to fully visualize, interact, and manipulate designs in a more immersive way. However, with the advent of AI-enhanced AR and VR technologies, this paradigm is changing, providing a much more intuitive, real-time, and spatial way to engage with digital designs.

NVIDIA Omniverse, a collaborative 3D simulation platform, serves as a key player in this transformation. By leveraging AI algorithms, NVIDIA Omniverse enables the seamless integration of CAD models into both AR and VR environments, allowing users to experience their designs in true three-dimensional space. This technology allows for much more than just visualization; it empowers real-time interaction, collaboration, and optimization of designs, all within a highly immersive and interactive 3D environment.

Through AI, the CAD models within these virtual environments are not simply static representations of designs but are enhanced by dynamic simulations, allowing users to experiment with design changes in a real-world context. This technology opens new frontiers in product development, enabling engineers and designers to test and refine their creations before physical prototypes are even made, which can dramatically reduce both development time and costs.

Real-Time Collaboration in 3D Environments

One of the most significant advantages of incorporating AR and VR into the CAD process is the ability to collaborate in real-time within a 3D environment. Traditional collaboration methods, which often rely on 2D drawings, static models, and text-based feedback, can be inefficient and prone to miscommunication. In contrast, with NVIDIA Omniverse, engineers, designers, and stakeholders can enter a shared virtual space where they can view and manipulate the same model simultaneously.

AI plays a crucial role in enhancing this collaborative experience by ensuring that all interactions within the virtual environment are accurately reflected in real-time. For instance, as one participant makes changes to a model, these changes are automatically synchronized and displayed to all other participants, ensuring that everyone is working with the most up-to-date version of the design. Furthermore, AI can automatically adjust the model's visual representation based on the context of the interaction, making it easier for users to interpret and evaluate different design elements.

Real-time collaboration becomes particularly valuable in multidisciplinary teams, where experts from various fields— such as mechanical, electrical, and industrial engineering— work together. Using AI-powered tools in Omniverse, these teams can view a design from different perspectives, make immediate adjustments, and provide instant feedback, all within a fully interactive 3D environment. This approach fosters better communication, accelerates decision-making, and reduces the chances of errors that may arise from misinterpretations of traditional 2D representations.

Digital Twins for Engineering Simulations

The concept of a digital twin—a virtual replica of a physical object or system—has gained considerable attention in industries such as manufacturing, aerospace, automotive, and construction. A digital twin allows engineers to create an exact virtual representation of a product or system that behaves in the same way as its physical counterpart. By incorporating AI, these digital twins become even more powerful, as they can continuously collect and analyze data from their physical counterparts to simulate real-time performance.

In the context of CAD and engineering simulations, AI-powered digital twins in NVIDIA Omniverse can provide highly accurate, real-time simulations of how a product will perform under various conditions. By integrating AI into this simulation process, the digital twin can adapt and evolve, incorporating new data or insights from past performance to offer more precise predictions and recommendations for design improvements.

For instance, AI can analyze how a particular CAD design will respond to external factors such as temperature changes, pressure variations, or wear and tear over time. The digital twin can simulate these conditions in real-time, providing engineers with the ability to test different scenarios without needing to create physical prototypes or conduct time-consuming physical tests. This capability not only enhances design accuracy but also allows for continuous optimization throughout the product lifecycle.

By connecting digital twins with AI-driven analytics, manufacturers can optimize their designs before they even enter production. This ensures that any flaws or inefficiencies in the product design can be detected early, saving both time and resources while improving overall product quality.

Visualizing and Interacting with a CAD Model

In this hands-on project, we will explore how AI-powered AR/VR integration in NVIDIA Omniverse allows users to interact with a CAD model in a fully immersive 3D environment. For this example, we will use a simple mechanical part, such as a gear assembly, to demonstrate the capabilities of Omniverse's AR/VR tools and how they can aid in the design and optimization process.

Step 1 Importing the CAD Model into Omniverse

The first step in this project is to import the CAD model of the gear assembly into the NVIDIA Omniverse platform. Omniverse supports a wide range of CAD formats, including those used by SolidWorks, Autodesk, and Rhino, making it easy to bring your existing designs into the platform. Once the model is imported, Omniverse automatically converts it into a format that can be manipulated in AR and VR environments.

Step 2 Setting Up the AR/VR Environment

Next, we will choose whether to work with AR or VR. If using AR, you can use a headset or a mobile device to overlay the CAD model into your physical environment. If using VR, you will be fully immersed in the digital space, interacting with the model as though it were a physical object in front of you. NVIDIA Omniverse allows both of these experiences to be seamlessly integrated into the platform, with the AI-driven environment adjusting based on the user's choice of interaction.

Step 3 Interaction and Visualization

Once inside the AR/VR environment, you can begin interacting with the model. Using the controllers or gestures in VR, or pointing and pinching in AR, you can zoom in, rotate, and manipulate the gear assembly in real-time. AI-powered features within Omniverse will enhance the user experience by providing context-aware tools. For example, as you zoom in on a specific area, the system might automatically highlight certain features or offer suggestions for improvements based on pre-existing simulation data.

Additionally, AI can simulate physical behaviors in real-time. As you interact with the assembly, AI algorithms can predict how different forces or conditions might affect the model, such as how the gears will perform under load. This kind of interactive simulation allows you to test design changes on the fly, making it possible to instantly assess how those changes might affect the performance or feasibility of the product.

Step 4 Real-Time Collaboration

If you are working in a collaborative environment, you can invite other team members to join the same AR/VR session. All participants can view the same model, interact with it, and make real-time changes. AI ensures that everyone in the session sees the most up-to-date version of the design, and it even allows the system to adjust the environment to each participant's preferences or role in the project. For instance, a designer might see the model from a high-level perspective, while a mechanical engineer might have more detailed access to the internal components.

Step 5 Optimizing the Design

After interacting with the model and receiving feedback from the AI-driven environment, you can apply design changes to optimize the gear assembly. For instance, the AI might suggest altering the geometry of the teeth to improve efficiency or proposing new materials for better durability. As these changes are made, the model is immediately updated, and you can visualize the new version of the design in the AR/VR environment.

This hands-on project demonstrates the power of AI in integrating CAD with AR and VR, allowing for a much more dynamic, immersive, and collaborative design process. By merging digital tools with the physical world, Omniverse enables a more intuitive approach to product design and simulation, paving the way for more innovative and efficient engineering processes.

AI integration with AR and VR through platforms like NVIDIA Omniverse is fundamentally transforming the way we approach CAD design and engineering simulations. By providing immersive environments, real-time collaboration, and AI-powered optimizations, this combination offers new ways for designers and engineers to visualize, interact with, and refine their work. As this technology continues to evolve, the boundaries between the physical and digital worlds will continue to blur, offering unprecedented possibilities for product development and innovation.

By engaging in these new AI-driven design workflows, engineers and designers can significantly improve productivity, enhance product quality, and reduce time to market. With tools like NVIDIA Omniverse, the future of CAD design is not only smarter but also more interactive, immersive, and collaborative than ever before.

Conclusion

In this book, we have explored a variety of AI-driven tools and their profound impact on engineering design, particularly within the realms of CAD (Computer-Aided Design) and 3D modeling. As technology advances, the integration of AI into design processes has not only enhanced the efficiency and precision of engineering but also transformed the way products are conceptualized, tested, and manufactured. Throughout this journey, we have examined the roles that AI plays in optimizing workflows, automating repetitive tasks, enabling real-time collaboration, and driving innovation in product design.

The tools discussed—from SolidWorks Xdesign for AI-powered 3D modeling and Ansys Discovery for AI-enhanced simulation and analysis, to Geomagic Design X for reverse engineering and nTopology for lattice structures—demonstrate the diverse ways AI can augment the design process. Each of these tools utilizes machine learning, data analysis, and real-time collaboration features to improve design accuracy, speed up prototyping, and reduce the likelihood of errors. Whether it's optimizing toolpaths for CNC machines, automating support structures for 3D printing, or creating photorealistic renderings in KeyShot AI, AI has proven to be a transformative force in engineering and manufacturing.

The Future of AI-Driven CAD

Looking toward the future, the role of AI in CAD and 3D modeling is only expected to grow more significant. With advancements in machine learning algorithms and greater computational power, we can expect more intelligent design tools capable of predicting design flaws before they even occur. AI will continue to assist in the creation of digital twins, enable real-time simulations, and facilitate design changes with unparalleled speed and accuracy. Moreover, AI-powered tools will likely become even more accessible, with more companies integrating AI into their everyday design workflows, allowing for greater democratization of advanced technologies in design and engineering fields.

The future of CAD and 3D modeling also holds exciting possibilities in the realm of customization. AI could enable the creation of fully personalized designs that are optimized for individual needs, preferences, or manufacturing constraints. As AI becomes more adept at understanding complex design problems and predicting the impact of various materials, geometries, and conditions, engineers will be able to push the boundaries of innovation even further, creating designs that are both functional and highly efficient. Additionally, the development of AI-enhanced AR and VR environments for collaboration will make it possible for teams to work on designs as if they were physical objects, providing an intuitive and immersive experience for engineers, designers, and stakeholders alike.

Furthermore, with the rise of generative design—where AI helps to automatically generate multiple design alternatives based on defined parameters—engineers will no longer be limited by traditional design approaches. Instead, they will have access to vast design possibilities, each one optimized for performance, cost, and material efficiency. This ability to create innovative and efficient designs in a fraction of the time previously required will significantly shorten development cycles, reduce costs, and enhance the competitiveness of industries.

Resources for Further Learning

As AI continues to revolutionize the field of engineering design, it is essential for professionals to stay ahead of the curve by continuously learning and adapting to new technologies. Below are some valuable resources for those interested in furthering their knowledge of AI-driven CAD and 3D modeling

Online Courses and Certifications Several online platforms offer specialized courses and certifications in AI, machine learning, CAD, and 3D modeling. Websites such as Coursera, edX, and Udemy provide access to courses on AI applications in design and engineering from top institutions like MIT, Stanford, and Autodesk.

Industry Conferences and Workshops Attending industry conferences such as the **Autodesk University** or the **SIGGRAPH Conference** provides opportunities to learn directly from industry experts about the latest AI-driven tools and techniques. These events often feature hands-on workshops and demonstrations, making them valuable for those who prefer a more interactive learning experience.

Academic Journals and Publications For in-depth research and the latest developments in AI-driven design, academic journals such as the **Journal of Artificial Intelligence in Engineering Design** and the **Computer-Aided Design Journal** offer peer-reviewed papers that explore cutting-edge AI technologies in engineering. These publications are excellent for staying informed about emerging trends and methodologies.

Software Vendor Documentation and Tutorials The developers of AI-driven design tools, such as **Autodesk**, **Dassault Systèmes (SolidWorks)**, and **PTC (Creo)**, provide extensive documentation, user manuals, and online tutorials for their software. These resources are invaluable for mastering the tools and gaining proficiency in their AI-driven features. Many of these platforms also offer community forums where users can exchange ideas, solve technical challenges, and discuss best practices.

Professional Associations and Networks Joining professional organizations such as the **American Society of Mechanical Engineers (ASME)**, **Society of Manufacturing Engineers (SME)**, and **International Association for the Engineering Analysis Community (NAFEMS)** can connect you with like-minded professionals and provide access to webinars, workshops, and networking events. These associations often have resources and events focused on AI and digital transformation in engineering.

Books and Educational Resources A wide range of books are available that focus on AI in engineering, machine learning, and CAD tools. Some highly recommended books include Artificial Intelligence for Engineers by Timothy P. McCarty and Designing with Data by Rochelle L. Eisenberg. These books provide both theoretical insights and practical advice on incorporating AI into the design process.

Hands-On Practice and Personal Projects Perhaps the best way to truly grasp the capabilities of AI in design is through hands-on practice. Many of the software platforms mentioned throughout the book, such as **SolidWorks**, **Ansys Discovery**, and **Fusion**

360, offer free trials or student versions that allow you to experiment with AI-enhanced tools. Setting up personal projects—whether it's designing a product, optimizing a part, or simulating a process—provides practical experience and deepens your understanding of how AI can be leveraged in design.

As AI continues to shape the landscape of CAD and 3D modeling, staying up to date with the latest trends and technologies will be crucial for engineers and designers looking to remain competitive. By actively engaging with these resources and continually learning, you can harness the power of AI to unlock new levels of innovation, efficiency, and precision in your design and engineering practices. In conclusion, the integration of AI into CAD and 3D modeling represents a significant leap forward in the field of engineering design. By automating complex tasks, enabling real-time collaboration, and enhancing the ability to predict and optimize designs, AI tools are helping engineers push the boundaries of what is possible. With the advancements discussed throughout this book, the future of design and manufacturing is undoubtedly intertwined with AI, creating opportunities for more efficient, innovative, and sustainable products. Through continuous learning and engagement with cutting-edge tools, professionals can position themselves at the forefront of this transformation and drive the future of engineering forward.

THE END